JOHN F. KENNEDY

A Life from Beginning to End

Copyright © 2017 by Hourly History

Table of Contents

Introduction

John F. Kennedy was born in a time when the memory of signs that said "No Irish Need Apply" were fresh in the minds of his family. He ran for president at a time when the concept of a Catholic in the Oval Office was inconceivable. His marriage to the beautiful, cultured Jacqueline Bouvier created an image of glamor that was very different from what post-war America was used to in its First Ladies. His womanizing was a secret kept from the public by a press that was complicit in the concealment.

Kennedy took office at a time in history when America and the world were both undergoing periods of dramatic social change. His inauguration promised so much hope for the future, but no historian has a crystal ball - and no one knows what he might have accomplished had he lived and been re-elected to serve a second term. Would he have acted upon his instincts that Vietnam was a quagmire, sparing the United States the division it suffered over the unpopular war that exposed the paranoia of a nation's obsession with stopping communism through CIA plots, war, and meddling in the governments of other nations? Could he have accomplished as much as his successor Lyndon B. Johnson did to promote civil rights and social justice? After proving himself through the tension of the Cuban Missile Crisis, would he have brought a new strength to dealings with the Soviet Union? Would the country, instead of losing itself in waves of violence and disenchantment with government, have found the inspiration in public service that Kennedy promoted?

We'll never know. Dallas robbed the nation of its hopes, delivering instead a multitude of images which are embedded in the nation's mental photo album: the smiling president and his beautiful wife riding in an open convertible; the Zapruder film images showing the impact of the bullets as Kennedy was shot; the swearing-in of Lyndon Johnson as president while the new First Lady and the widow, still wearing her blood-stained pink suit, witnessed another page in history's traumatic book of events; Walter Cronkite giving way to emotion as he revealed to the nation that the President had died; the awe-inspiring, somber funeral that the First Lady planned, even as she planned a birthday party for her young son, determinedly forging on with her duties as a mother and her responsibilities to her fallen husband.

In 1964, Jackie's pink suit and the accessories she wore on that terrible day were sent to the National Archives. In 2103, the dress was made available for viewing by the public, according to the instructions of Caroline Kennedy Schlossberg, the daughter of John Fitzgerald Kennedy and Jacqueline Bouvier Kennedy. What will that pink suit, marred with bloodstains, mean to the Americans of that time? Will the events of November 23 still resonate in the national consciousness when no one is alive who can recall what he or she was doing on that fateful day in Dallas? The Kennedys were icons on a grand stage, and the pink suit is as much an icon of American history as is Marilyn Monroe serenading the president on his birthday, his charge to the nation to ask not what your country can do for you, but what you can do for your country, and the riderless horse at his funeral. The images never fade.

Kennedy the President was the conclusion of a book made up of many chapters, the privileged son born to an ambitious scion of immigrants who defied the prejudice against the Irish. He was ill from childhood, yet he personified the image of a man of indomitable strength. As a man, he was far from flawless, but perhaps the fairest way to judge him is to recognize that his presidency embodied the hopes of a nation founded on lofty ideals. America, and JFK, did not always reach those exalted heights, but the man and the nation he led never stopped believing in them.

Chapter One

No Irish Need Apply

"When my great-grandfather left here to become a cooper in East Boston, he carried nothing with him except two things - a strong religious faith and a strong desire for liberty."

—John F. Kennedy

The nineteenth century saw a mass exodus of Irish immigrants fleeing desperate poverty and oppression in their native country to try their luck in the United States. Two of those immigrants, Patrick Kennedy and Bridget Murphy, left County Wexford for Boston, marrying in 1849. Bridget Murphy Kennedy, whose eldest son had died of cholera, became a widow when Patrick died in a cholera epidemic, leaving her with a son, Patrick Joseph. As a businesswoman who owned a store that later grew into a grocery and liquor store, she was able to provide her son with a formal education, the first Kennedy to receive one. When the boy was fourteen years old, he left school and went to work on the docks in Boston. He had inherited his mother's business acumen, and he saved his money so that he could buy a saloon, and then a second one. A third one, this one in a Boston hotel that serviced the upper classes, was purchased next. From saloons, he expanded to importing whiskey.

Prosperity brought better real estate so that he could move his family—by then he was married—to East Boston, where his neighbors included not only Irish Catholics who, like him, had risen above the poverty of their origins, but also Protestants of influence. Kennedy decided that it wasn't enough to just be a businessman; he wanted to be a politician. In 1884, he ran for the first of five consecutive terms as a member of the House of Representatives in Massachusetts and three two-year terms in the state senate. Politics seemed to be in the blood of the Irish, but Kennedy found that what he really wanted was to become a mover and shaker in the Boston political machine, pulling strings for the other candidates.

His oldest child, Joseph Patrick Kennedy, was born in 1888 in circumstances very different from those that his father had risen from. P.J. Kennedy had the advantage of going to school until age 14, but his son Joseph Kennedy went to Harvard College, and, upon graduation with a degree in economics, became a bank examiner. When the bank in which his father was a shareholder was at risk of being taken over, Kennedy borrowed the money he needed to take control and by the age of twenty-five was the bank president. He was in his twenties when he began to make his reputation and his fortune in the stock market as an investor,

The Irish had been in Massachusetts long enough to have their own society, and the Kennedys were at the top of the social pyramid. Another prominent Irish Catholic family was the Fitzgeralds. Rose Fitzgerald had been educated in the Netherlands, studied piano at the New England Conservatory, and attended the Manhattanville College of the Sacred Heart before she and her father, the outgoing, irrepressible John Francis "Honey Fitz" Fitzgerald, toured Europe. For Rose, her Catholic faith was an innate part of her character, a source of strength for her during a long life that saw more than its share of tragedy and trial.

In 1914, the families were joined when Joseph Kennedy married Rose Fitzgerald. The marriage produced nine children: Joseph Patrick Jr; John Fitzgerald; Rosemary; Kathleen; Eunice; Patricia; Robert, Jean, and Edward. Their father expected great things from his children, and each one had a story to tell, but the Kennedys were Irish and Catholic, and the nation was grounded in the primacy of the Protestant elite, making Joseph Kennedy's social aspirations seem foolish.

Kennedy vowed that before he was thirty-five years old, he intended to make a million dollars. The 1929 stock market crash didn't damage the family's wealth; Kennedy had become a multi-millionaire during the booming 1920s and prospered during the Depression; the canny Irishman credited his sense of timing with his prosperity, and by 1935 he was worth $180 million. He was a rich man, but he was still an Irish Catholic. The money came readily, but it wasn't enough to have money: Kennedy wanted power as well.

The patriarch of the Kennedy clan was, like his father before him, was not only a businessman but also involved in politics. He supported the candidacy of Franklin Delano Roosevelt in the 1932 presidential election, but his campaigning and support didn't lead to the Cabinet position he coveted. Instead, he was named the chairman of the Securities and Exchange Commission, using his background knowledge of the banking industry to bring about reforms.

The children of Joseph and Rose Kennedy lived lives of privilege, protected from the privation of the Depression years; John Kennedy admitted that he had no personal experience of the grueling years of the Depression and only knew about it from the books he read when he was a student at Harvard.

The Kennedys lived in a spacious home outside of Boston. They spent their summers in Hyannis Port. They were an energetic, active, and competitive family whose zeal to win at sports was encouraged by their father. The competition between the two oldest boys, Joe Jr. and Jack, was intense, and Joe Jr. generally emerged the victor.

But John Kennedy, who was named after his maternal grandfather, John Francis Fitzgerald, did not have an easy life. He was a sickly boy, and Rose Kennedy, who kept notecards which recorded the growth and developments of her children, noted that during his childhood he had chicken pox, whooping cough, and measles. A bout of scarlet fever when he was three years old was serious enough to threaten his life, and his father visited him the hospital every day for the month that the boy was a patient there. Illness didn't keep him from engaging in school activities, however; when he was a student at Choate, he enjoyed team sports like football and basketball, but also solo sports like golf and tennis. As a student, he subscribed to the New York Times and preferred the subjects of history and English. His father wrote to him that he felt his son wasn't living up to his promise and that he needed to work harder.

Following in the Kennedy footsteps, in 1936 Jack went to Harvard as his father had, and where brother Joe was a student. Illness followed Jack to college, leading to a lasting problem when he ruptured a disk in his spine during a game of football. The injury would trouble him throughout his adult life. He was an average student, but what he lacked in academic prowess he made up for in his awareness of the world situation. The thirties were a precarious decade in Europe, and Jack Kennedy's travels abroad gave him insights into the threats looming on the horizon.

He lacked a scholarly touch, but he had a flair for writing. When he was a senior, he wrote his thesis examining why Great Britain was not alert to the war threat. His professors gave the thesis high marks, but his proud and ambitious father thought it could be more and he encouraged publication. The book, entitled *Why England Slept*, was published in 1940, and *Time* magazine's Henry Luce agreed to write the foreword. Although Jack was credited as the author, the thesis underwent some rewriting in order to become a book, and there's long been a belief that the final product was less the work of a Harvard senior than the work of Arthur Krock, a former *New York Times* bureau chief.

However, Joseph Kennedy was content to have a son who was a writer. Eldest son Joseph had already convinced his family that he was going to become the first Irish-Catholic president of the United States.

Chapter Two

War and the Kennedys

"When asked what I am most proud of, I stick out my chest, hold my head high, and state proudly, 'I served in the United States Navy!'"

—John F. Kennedy

Ambassadorships have long been the plum jobs awarded to political supporters, and in 1937 Franklin Roosevelt appointed Joseph Kennedy as the Ambassador to the Court of St. James's, the official name of the ambassadorship to the United Kingdom. The Kennedy brood moved to England while the oldest boys were at Harvard. Nazism and Fascism had placed Adolf Hitler and Benito Mussolini in charge of Germany and Italy, and the rest of Europe, well aware that the Axis leaders coveted more land and power, waited nervously to see what would happen next. In 1939, they had their answer: Germany conquered Poland, and Europe was at war.

The Ambassador opposed the United States going into war, but that didn't stop his sons from enlisting. Jack Kennedy's bad back and other health issues initially caused him to be rejected from service, but his father pulled strings so that his son could join up. Both joined the Navy. Lieutenant John Kennedy was named commander of PT-109, a patrol torpedo boat in the South Pacific. The mission of Kennedy and his 12-man crew was to prevent Japanese ships from bringing supplies to their soldiers. Kennedy's boat was one of fifteen assigned to block the convoy of supplies that were delivered on a regular basis from the Japanese navy, which was combatting American forces advancing from the south. The delivery vessels were known to the American troops as the Tokyo Express.

On patrol as usual on the night of August 2, 1943, the crew suddenly found itself in the path of a Japanese destroyer—one of four as part of the transport crew—moving too fast for the PT boat to get out of the way. The destroyer struck the boat, splitting it in half. Two members of the crew were killed; the others jumped off the boat before it erupted in flames. They didn't see any sign of the other PT boats and they didn't dare fire their flare guns because of the risk of alerting the Japanese ships surrounding the islands. Some of the crew were clinging to a piece of the boat that had remained afloat; Kennedy, although his back had been injured when the impact of the collision slammed him against the cockpit, led the crew to an island a few miles away, towing an injured member by gripping the life jacket strap between his teeth. Kennedy's past participation on the Harvard swim team came to his aid, and several members of his crew were also skilled swimmers. However, two members couldn't swim, so they had to be tied to a plank that the crew pushed forward.

They reached the island. Jack was exhausted and needed help from the sailor he had towed. He wanted to see if he could attract another PT boat, but after swimming out into the route where the boats traveled and treading water for an hour, he realized that they were alone. Swimming against the current on his trip back, he stopped on another island just to sleep so that he'd have enough strength to make it back to his crew.

They ventured out for food and water but only found coconuts. Greater exploration wasn't possible because of the prevalence of the Japanese patrols, but further exploring the next day led them to a tin of water, a box containing

Japanese candy, and a canoe concealed in the bushes. When they were discovered by natives, the crew realized they had hopes of a rescue.

In order to communicate the situation, Kennedy carved a message on a coconut shell:

Nauru Island

Commander

Native knows posit He can pilot 11 alive need small boat

More islanders showed up with food for the crew, along with instructions from the Allies who had received the message they had delivered. On August 8, the crew was rescued and brought to a U.S. base.

Jack was a war hero and received medals from the Navy and Marine Corps for his bravery, and a Purple Heart for his injuries. *The New Yorker* and *Reader's Digest* reported on the story. Jack's heroism was the silver lining of the dark cloud that encased the Kennedys during the war years. Kathleen Kennedy, known as Kick, had become romantically involved with William Cavendish, a titled Englishman who was a Protestant. Her mother disapproved of the relationship, and when Kathleen and William were married on May 6, 1944, the only Kennedy to attend the ceremony was her older brother Joseph Jr.

Joe Jr. had been a student at Harvard Law School when he left to enlist in the United States Naval Reserve in June 1941, six months before the U.S. would enter the war. As a naval aviator, he completed twenty-five combat missions and had the option of returning home. Instead, he volunteered for a secret mission known as Operation Aphrodite. Joe Jr.'s plane exploded, killing the eldest Kennedy son.

Joe Jr. was awarded the Purple Heart, the Navy Cross, and the Air Medal posthumously. His name was listed on the Tablets of the Missing at the Cambridge American

Cemetery in Great Britain that honors the sacrifice of American servicemen who lost their lives in World War II. Ironically, Joe Jr. would be the only Kennedy son who would not be a presidential candidate.

With Joe Jr.'s death, the second son was the hope of the family's ambitions, but Jack Kennedy's physical health, which had been compromised since his childhood, showed more evidence of weakness after his war experience. However, theories that the back problems that were part of his persona stemmed from his PT-109 experience have been refuted; research shows that his vertebrae possibly began degenerating in the 1930s when he started taking steroids to address severe diarrhea that today would likely have been diagnosed as irritable bowel syndrome. Physical health would always be a matter of concern for the young man who, throughout his life, sought to project a vigorous, energetic image despite near constant pain; his brother, who had not suffered from ill health, was gone.

Joe Jr.'s death was more than a family tragedy. It also meant that the destiny that his father had planned now passed to the second son. Joseph Kennedy intended to have a son who would be the first Irish Catholic president of the United States. With the death of Joe, Jr., the mantle fell to the second son, John Fitzgerald Kennedy.

Chapter Three

Kennedy in Congress

"When we (The Democrats) got into office, the thing that surprised me most was to find that things were just as bad as we'd been saying they were."

—John F. Kennedy

After the war, Jack Kennedy had to figure out his future direction. His father, ever mindful of the political destiny he coveted, wanted his son for Congress. The charming war hero with the engaging smile won the election in 1946 and would serve three terms as the representative for the Massachusetts Eleventh Congressional District. Joe Kennedy had a long political reach in Boston, and when he suggested that Representative James Michael Curley might like being the mayor of Boston again—he'd previously served three terms in the position and remained popular with Irish Catholic voters who were unconcerned that he'd also served prison time for fraud, bribery, and other standard political vices that were a mainstay of party politics—Curley vacated his congressional seat in 1946. The seat was located in a district that was strongly Democratic, and Jack Kennedy, just twenty-nine years old, beat his Republican opponent easily.

He entered Congress at a time when the Republicans controlled the House of Representatives. Jack Kennedy had no intentions of remaining in the House for long, but while he was there, he concentrated on providing satisfaction for the people of his district. He was also mindful of the needs of returning veterans and concentrated on trying to move a bill forward that would make affordable housing available for the GIs who came back from war. The cause was a popular one; veterans needed the help, and the members of his district wanted a government that helped them, not one that preached about the kind of fiscal conservatism that Kennedy was more aligned with.

Joseph Kennedy knew that in order for his son to become a national figure, Congress was a necessary stepping stone to higher office. He provided the funds for Jack to put together a top staff both in his Massachusetts district and at his Washington D.C. office.

Knowing that he was unlikely to be victorious in a Senate run in 1948, Jack ran for re-election to the House and was victorious for a second and third term. Like many Americans, Kennedy had emerged from World War II with an overwhelming suspicion of the Soviet Union and a distrust of communism. In Kennedy's opinion, President Harry Truman wasn't doing everything he should have done to combat the menace, a stance which Joe McCarthy adopted and turned into a national witch hunt. Kennedy avoided the extremism of McCarthy, although he was not unsympathetic to some of the Wisconsin Republican senator's concerns. McCarthy's crusade against communism would be an obsessive quest to out sympathizers in government, the military, and the arts, creating a suspicious atmosphere in which patriotism took on an ominous tone. The war that had just been won was setting the stage for a Cold War between the superpowers of the United States and the Soviet Union, one which would engage all politicians on various levels for a generation.

His stance was one which would resonate with voters, but the 11th District wasn't big enough for Kennedy's ambitions and the dogged pace of legislation in the House was too slow for him. He began to plan his campaign for a Senate race, which meant making his mark on a wider audience. The Korean War was underway, and Kennedy wanted to see how this would affect the defense of Western Europe, to which the United States was committed. He also visited Vietnam, where he expressed opposition to the support that the U.S. was providing to the French in the area, criticizing the French for their imperial intentions. Upon his return, he testified before Senate committees and other audiences as well.

The 1952 campaign for the Senate was a tale of two Bostons. Henry Cabot Lodge, the Republican candidate, represented the Old Guard: wealthy, Protestant, with a pedigree that went back to Puritan forebears in the seventeenth century. Kennedy, the Democrat, was Irish, Catholic, and young at age 35. The country was changing, and so was the Massachusetts power base, but it wasn't all demographics; there was a personal element as well. In 1916, Henry Cabot Lodge's grandfather beat Honey Fitz in the race for the Senate.

Jack Kennedy knew he had a battle in store. He campaigned by visiting every town in Massachusetts before the day of the election. Rose Kennedy and the Kennedy sisters hosted tea parties with the candidate as a guest so that the ladies had a chance to meet the candidate. An estimated 70,000 guests attended these tea parties.

Perhaps Lodge was confident that Kennedy was a lightweight opponent. He was busy encouraging World War II General Dwight D. Eisenhower to run for the presidency, even though there were many who felt that well-known Ohio Senator Robert Taft was the rightful candidate. Taft supporters were angry at Lodge for his failure to throw his weight behind Taft.

Working behind the scenes, Joseph Kennedy was determined to do whatever needed to be done in order to help his son win. The *Boston Post* intended to endorse Lodge. Knowing that the newspaper was in financial trouble, the Kennedy patriarch obtained a loan for half a million dollars to stabilize the newspaper. The endorsement went to Kennedy.

The Republican candidate for president, Dwight D. Eisenhower, won Massachusetts, but Kennedy beat Lodge for the state's Senate seat by 70,000 votes - the same number of people who attended the Kennedy women's tea parties. The margin of victory was narrow, and election returns kept the candidate guessing until 5:00 the following morning, but the victory was significant.

Kennedy did not intend his Senate victory to be his last political achievement, but bouts of bad health prevented him from pursuing his role as a senator with full engagement. He had been diagnosed with Addison's disease in the 1940s, a condition of the adrenal glands that causes them to fail to produce enough steroid hormones. Symptoms of fatigue, dizziness, weight loss, and mood changes were typical of the disease; the effects of the disease once caused him to collapse when he was on a congressional visit to Great Britain. The family kept his medical history a secret, unwilling to admit just how ill he was. The young man, who seemed so carefree and energetic, had a health resume that would have downed a less determined man: appendicitis, jaundice, hepatitis, and malaria, as well as having problems hearing in his left ear and being allergic to dogs. In fact, Kennedy was so ill that he received the last rites three times during his life.

His back problems were well known and were not kept secret. His back woes may have stemmed from the steroids he had taken, prescribed by doctors at a time when the medical field failed to realize how severely long-term use of corticosteroids could affect physical health. In 1954, despite the fact that no one with Addison's disease had survived traumatic surgery, Kennedy had an operation on his back because of the terrific pain he was suffering. The surgery was serious enough, but his hospitalization lasted for nine months because he also incurred a urinary tract infection and a reaction to the blood transfusion.

While in the hospital, Kennedy returned to his writing. The book, *Profiles in Courage*, explored the careers of Senators John Quincy Adams, Daniel Webster, Thomas Hart Benton, Sam Houston, Edmund G. Ross, Lucius Lamar, George Norris, and Robert Taft, all of whom took stances which were unpopular with the public because they believed it was the right thing to do. The book won the Pulitzer Prize in 1957, but in truth, Kennedy didn't do most of the writing. That achievement belonged to his aide and friend, Ted Sorenson. Syndicated columnist Drew Pearson first made the accusation that Kennedy was not the author of the book in 1957 when he appeared on an ABC television show. Kennedy threatened to sue the network and ABC retracted Pearson's comment. Once again, the credit—or blame—for the book may rest with the string-pulling Joseph Kennedy, who knew that a popular, award-winning book could not hurt his son's chances for higher office.

When he—and his crutches—returned to the Senate, Jack Kennedy participated on the Select Committee of the Senate to Investigate Improper Activities in Labor-Management Relations. His younger brother Robert, in his role as chief counsel, was investigating charges of labor union officials involved in racketeering.

By the time of the 1956 presidential election, Kennedy's fame had reached the point where he was almost the Democratic candidate for vice president. He was re-elected to the Senate in 1958, but by that time, he had no interest in being vice president. He intended to run for president.

Chapter Four

Kennedy for President

"I should have remembered that 'a picture is worth a thousand words.'"

—Richard Nixon

The 1960 presidential election was not a contest between two politicians with dramatically different ideologies. The men were close in age; Richard Nixon was forty-seven years old, Kennedy forty-three. They were both veterans of World War II and had seen the remarkable transformation of the United States into a world power. However, the world power had a challenger, and voters were jittery at the prospect of the Soviet Union overtaking the U.S. Richard Nixon could point to the peace and prosperity of the Eisenhower presidency and promise that Ike's vice president was able to continue the pattern of security, thanks to Nixon's experience. That stability was enhanced by his choice of running mate, Henry Cabot Lodge, the man who had surrendered his Senate seat to Kennedy in 1952.

John Kennedy's air of youthfulness was a stark contrast to Nixon, despite the fact that only four years separated the two men in age. Kennedy had life experience, but his foreign affairs knowledge was limited in terms of governing - and he was Catholic. There had never been a Catholic president in the United States. The status quo versus change. Still, other things were changing in the world.

The Soviets had already made the leap into space before the Americans when they launched Sputnik in 1957, and the struggle for supremacy was no longer earthbound. Cuba's revolutionary leader, Fidel Castro, flaunted his ties to the Soviets. Was America falling behind? Was war with the Soviet Union looming? On the home front, what was the struggle for civil rights portend for the future of the country?

Kennedy proposed a series of debates between the candidates, a suggestion which was not popular with Nixon's advisors. The growth of the new medium of television had exploded by 1960, with 88 percent of the homes in America owning a television. Even Eisenhower thought it was a mistake to give Kennedy more national exposure voluntarily, but Nixon was confident of his ability to make his case for leadership over his Democratic opponent.

Kennedy proved himself to be more media savvy than Nixon. The studio had a gray background, so Kennedy wore a blue suit and shirt, which diminished the glare of the lights; Nixon wore a gray suit that blended into the set. The Kennedy-Nixon debate, a harbinger of the way that the new, visual medium would revolutionize voter perceptions, has since become part of television legend: a young-looking, vigorous Kennedy defeated a sweaty, pale Nixon; Kennedy faced the camera and by extension, the American public; Nixon looked at the reporters while answering the debate questions. However, the truth was a little more layered. Kennedy's tan may have come from his time outdoors campaigning, but some believe that he may have had help from make-up; the view has also been expressed that his complexion was one of the results of Addison's disease. Nixon put on pancake makeup to conceal his stubble, but the powder melted under the lights. After the debate, Nixon's mother called the candidate to ask him if wasn't feeling well.

The damage was done. Listeners to the debate who weren't distracted by the visual impressions because they tuned in via radio believed that Nixon won the debate; viewers said Kennedy won.

The election was destined to be a tight race. Kennedy was a skilled campaigner who appealed to voters looking for a change. Nixon's experience didn't seem to be as compelling to voters as he'd expected it to be. Kennedy, who had been challenged on the basis of his Catholicism by the entrenched Old Guard, who felt that a Roman Catholic president would be ruled by the Pope, countered that fear when he addressed the Greater Houston Ministerial Association. Kennedy treated the issue not as a personal one but as a constitutional concern, answering, "I believe in an America that is officially neither Catholic, Protestant nor Jewish; where no public official either requests or accepts instructions on public policy from the Pope, the National Council of Churches or any other ecclesiastical source; where no religious body seeks to impose its will directly or indirectly upon the general populace or the public acts of its officials; and where religious liberty is so indivisible that an act against one church is treated as an act against all."

The early returns showed Kennedy with a lead from voters in the Northeast and the urban Midwest, but Nixon was winning the rural states and the West. Although Kennedy ended up winning the Electoral College votes 303 to 219, the popular vote showed him the victor by a mere 0.17%. There were accusations of fraud, particularly in Texas, the home state of Kennedy's running mate, Lyndon B. Johnson, and in Illinois, where Mayor Richard Daley's political influence was renowned for its power and occasional willingness to bend the rules.

Whatever the source, the results were clear: Joseph Kennedy had gotten his wish. His son was the 35th president of the United States, the youngest man elected to the presidency and the first person born in the 20th century to become president.

As he said in his speech when he was inaugurated on January 20, 1961, the torch had been passed to a new generation. He acknowledged the problems that lay before him: the tyranny of communism and the bondage of those peoples who lived under its oppression; the deadliness of the arms race and the inherent threat of annihilation; the chains of poverty. In recognizing the dangers that he would face in his leadership, he challenged Americans to answer the need in stirring words that summoned citizens to public service. "Ask not what your country can do for you; ask what you can do for your country. My fellow citizens of the world, ask not what America will do for you, but what together we can do for the Freedom of Man."

The speech, just 1,364 words, only lasted thirteen minutes and was the fourth-shortest of all presidential inauguration speeches, but it's regarded by historians as one of the most effective and stirring inaugural addresses in the history of the American presidency. Kennedy certainly had able speechwriters to help him deliver his message. He also had the ability to select words that would let his oratory soar, lifting the passages from the page so that they could take flight in the consciousness of the public.

It was a new decade and a new post-war era, but as Americans watched their new president take the oath of office, they may have recognized that their world was changing and the Kennedys were a symbol of that change. Attending the inauguration were the expected dignitaries, including former First Ladies Edith Wilson and Eleanor Roosevelt, and former President Harry Truman. Also in attendance were writers John Steinbeck and Ernest

Hemingway; poet Robert Frost recited his poem as part of the ceremony. A new appreciation for culture and the arts was showcased, but not all of the celebration was highbrow. The night before the inauguration, Kennedy's Rat Pack pals Frank Sinatra and Peter Lawford (who was married to Kennedy's sister Patricia) hosted a ball featuring appearances by Hollywood heavyweights like Sidney Poitier, Gene Kelly, Nat King Cole, Milton Berle, and others.

Hollywood and haute couture would fare well in the new administration's public side. The President and his beautiful, stylish and sophisticated First Lady were the main characters in what would become known as Camelot. The Broadway musical of the same name was a smash hit and the Kennedys enjoyed the music. It was easy, in the heady early days of the presidency, to forget that Camelot was also the story of a tragedy.

Chapter Five

Kennedy Women

"Because of my father, I was used to infidelities, but Jack's womanizing hurt me greatly."

—Jacqueline Kennedy

When John Kennedy entered the Senate, he was a bachelor - and an extremely eligible one. The public posture of the Kennedy men and their commitment to Catholicism did not mean that they were saints. Joseph Kennedy Sr. may have fathered nine children with wife Rose, but he was famous for his infidelities, most notably with Hollywood actress Gloria Swanson.

John Kennedy had been sexually promiscuous as far back as his days when he was a high school student at Choate. When he was a Navy ensign in 1941, he was involved with a Danish journalist named Inga Arvad who was rumored to be a Nazi spy because she had interviewed Adolf Hitler in 1935. The FBI was so concerned about Arvad's reputed Nazi connections that Director J. Edgar Hoover had her under surveillance and used devices to eavesdrop when she and Kennedy were alone because the FBI feared that she was using Kennedy to obtain information about the American Navy. There was no evidence that anything of that nature was happening, but Kennedy was reassigned to South Carolina and the relationship ended.

In 1952, Kennedy attended a dinner party in Washington D.C. where he met Jacqueline Bouvier, an inquiring photographer for the *Washington Times-Herald*. Bouvier, who had graduated from George Washington University with a degree in French literature, was the daughter of a hard-drinking stockbroker and a socialite who had divorced. Jacqueline had attended the Sorbonne in Paris as an exchange student; before entering college, she had been named "debutante of the year" by Igor Cassini when she made her debut. Like Kennedy, she was a Catholic and, through her mother, of Irish descent. Both of them appreciated literature and culture, and both benefitted from a worldlier, more sophisticated outlook, which grew out of their time spent abroad, but because of his campaigning for his Senate seat, Kennedy didn't have much time for wooing. However, after he won his seat, he proposed marriage. Bouvier was assigned to cover Queen Elizabeth's coronation and spent a month in Europe. When she returned, her answer was yes. As was typical of the times when wives didn't work outside the home, she resigned her job at the newspaper.

Archbishop Richard Cushing married the pair on September 12, 1953, in Newport, Rhode Island. There were 700 guests at the ceremony and 1200 at the reception, making the marriage one of the season's most celebrated social events. After honeymooning in Acapulco, the newlyweds lived in McLean, Virginia. Kennedy's health issues continued into his marriage, and he had back surgery the year after their wedding. In 1955, Jacqueline had a miscarriage; she gave birth to a stillborn daughter in 1956. They sold the McLean house to Robert and Ethel Kennedy, who already had a growing family, and moved to Georgetown.

Finally, in 1957, the Kennedys had a daughter, Caroline. *Life* magazine had the young family on its cover in 1958, publicity that didn't hurt Kennedy's campaign for re-election to the Senate. What surprised everyone was

Jacqueline's popularity among the crowds who showed up to see Kennedy; the crowds were twice as large when she was there. Jacqueline was not a natural campaigner; unlike her husband, she disliked media attention and was shy in the company of strangers.

She was not willing to be the typical politician's wife, but she was smart in her assessments and supportive of Kennedy's ambitions. She knew that next on the agenda was a run for the presidency, but when she became pregnant, her campaigning had to be curtailed because of her previous complications.

She was both an asset and a problem for the campaign. Her elegance and appeal made her a media sensation, but her fashion sense and a fondness for French dress designers aroused talk about the amount of money that she spent on her clothes.

The election was expected to be close, but Kennedy defeated Vice President Richard Nixon in 1960. Just over two weeks later, the Kennedys welcomed their son, John Fitzgerald Kennedy, Jr., while the public and the media attended to the story with fascination. The White House in recent years had been the residence of older presidents and First Ladies; there hadn't been young children in the White House since Teddy Roosevelt and his brood in the early years of the 20th century. The Kennedys brought their own youth, a young family, and an atmosphere of culture that transformed Washington D.C.

Her family came first, but the First Lady's interest in history led her to restore the White House, searching for historic furniture that would enhance the appeal of the nation's residence. She began by improving the attractiveness of the family's living quarters, which used up the $50,000 allocated for the project. Restoring the White House would take more money than Congress was likely to appropriate, however. Funds were raised by the sale of a

White House guidebook. Mrs. Kennedy, searching authentic furnishings which belonged to the White House, contacted donors. The habit had been for presidents to take furniture with them when their terms ended, but Kennedy initiated a bill to ensure that the furnishings remained when the presidents left, establishing the items as property of the Smithsonian Institution.

The First Lady's commitment to history overcame her dislike of publicity. In 1962, she allowed CBS News to film her giving a tour of the White House, which was viewed by more than 56 million Americans. Her efforts earned her an Emmy Award, making her the only First Lady to be so honored. Her appeal was strong in the U.S., but also in the rest of the world. She was bilingual, and on trips to France and Mexico, she spoke in the native languages of those countries.

The Kennedys once again faced tragedy when a son, Patrick Bouvier, was born prematurely in August 1963 and died two days after birth. The death would deeply affect Jacqueline Kennedy and send her into depression, but it also had the effect of solidifying the Kennedy marriage, which had endured not only the failed pregnancies but also her husband's infidelities.

Kennedy was not merely unfaithful to his wife; he was also indiscreet in his choices. One of his reputed mistresses, Judith Campbell Exner, had been introduced to Senator Kennedy in 1960 by Frank Sinatra. Not long after, she became the mistress of Mafia boss Sam Giancana, but when Exner was subpoenaed by the Senate Church Committee on Government Operations and Intelligence years later, she denied knowing anything about any connection between Kennedy and the Mafia.

Perhaps more notorious was Kennedy's affair with 1960s sex symbol and actress Marilyn Monroe. The two met at a dinner party in 1962 and, according to other guests, the chemistry was apparent. What was an affair for the amorous president was more heartfelt for the troubled actress. Her breathy, sensuous singing of "Happy Birthday" to Kennedy ignited gossip about the relationship, and Kennedy didn't want his infidelities to become public fodder. He cooled toward her but she failed to realize that the affair was over, even calling the White House to reach him until Kennedy was obliged to send a friend to deliver the news that the goodbye was for real. Womanizing was a pastime, but governing was his calling.

Chapter Six

The Presidency

"The most sweeping and forthright (proposals) ever presented by an American president."

—Martin Luther King, Jr.

John Kennedy succeeded to the presidency at a time when the youth culture was rising to pre-eminence. Music, movies, dances, and fashion all demonstrated that the 20th century was in the throes of dynamic change. One of his first acts as president was to acknowledge the optimism of his presidency and his faith in youth by creating the Peace Corps in March 1961 to recruit volunteers who would serve their nation's best ideals by working all over the world in education, agriculture, healthcare, and other fields.

However, it was early in his presidency when he faced a crisis not of his making. Cuban leader Fidel Castro's leadership was an affront to the CIA and to the Cuban exiles in the United States. On April 17, 1961, a paramilitary group sponsored by the CIA attempted to invade the island with the goal of overthrowing Castro and his government, but the attempt failed; after three days, the invasion was repelled by the Cuban military under the command of Castro. Castro's ties to the Soviet Union would be strengthened, planting the seeds for another Cuban crisis to come in Kennedy's presidency. The failure of the invasion was humiliating for the United States and an embarrassing introduction to Kennedy's grasp of foreign policy. At a press conference, Kennedy accepted blame for the failure. Castro's brother Raul concurred with that assessment, saying that if Kennedy had been resolved to invade, the Cuban revolution could have been destroyed. The time would soon come when Kennedy's resolve would not falter when confronting Cuba.

The domestic problems with which Kennedy would wrestle had longstanding roots. The Civil Rights Act had been signed into law in 1957 by President Eisenhower, but a law on paper could not easily counteract the tradition of segregation which ruled the Jim Crow South. On October 1, 1962, James Meredith, an African-American Air Force veteran, applied to be a student at the University of Mississippi. The state's governor opposed Meredith's aim to study at Ole Miss. Kennedy sent in federal troops and U.S. Marshals. Eventually, Meredith would graduate in 1963, but the rioting, death, and violence warned that the struggle for equal rights for all Americans would not be achieved without a fight.

It was destined to be a memorable autumn. On October 14 of that same year, Kennedy learned that CIA spy planes had spotted evidence that the Soviet Union was installing missile sites on Cuba. Kennedy realized that this threat could bring on a nuclear war, but he also faced an internal dilemma. Some of his advisors wanted an attack on the missile sites, but other advisors reminded Kennedy that the United States had missiles in Italy and Turkey, which had been placed there under Eisenhower's administration.

Speaking on television, Kennedy announced to the nation that he had informed the Soviet Union's Premier Nikita Khrushchev that the United States had established a naval quarantine with the intention of inspecting all Soviet ships trying to enter Cuban waters. The United Nations suggested that the United States end the quarantine so that tensions could ease between the two nations. Kennedy, mindful of the fact that Khrushchev thought him weak, refused. The world was closer to nuclear war than it had ever been. Finally, after a Soviet ship was boarded, Khrushchev agreed to dismantle the sites. The United States vowed that it would never invade Cuba and quietly agreed to move the missiles in Italy and Turkey.

The world was impressed by Kennedy's steely resolve; the nation was proud of its young president who had inherited a number of potential problems from the Eisenhower years. One of those problems was in Southeast Asia, where the Cold War was being carried out by proxy. Kennedy's policies continued to support the government of South Vietnam against the communist North Vietnam, which was supported by the Soviet Union. After the Viet Cong had become a stronger adversary against South Vietnam, Kennedy increased the number of Special Forces in the country; still, he resisted deploying troops on a larger scale. Kennedy analyzed the situation and realized that, as he put it, the United States "didn't have a prayer of staying in Vietnam. Those people hate us." However, Kennedy could not risk letting the communists win. The Vietnam War would escalate, and a Kennedy advisor later described it as "the only foreign policy problem handed off by JFK . . . in no better, and possibly worse shape than it was when he inherited it."

The Cold War was fought on various fronts. It was fought in space as the United States and the Soviet Union competed for supremacy with rockets. It was fought in Cuba. One of the earliest fronts was in Europe, particularly in Berlin, the divided city. The Soviet Union controlled East Berlin, and a wall separated the two sections of the city. In June 1963, Kennedy traveled to West Berlin and delivered a resounding defense of democracy when he stated, "Freedom has many difficulties and democracy is not perfect, but we have never had to put up a wall to keep our people in." Stating his support and the support of the world for the people of Berlin, Kennedy said, "Ich bin ein Berliner." The Berlin Wall would not fall for several more decades, but Kennedy's stance confirmed that its presence was a symbol of communist oppression.

Back home, the battle fought by African-Americans to achieve their constitutional right to equality continued to be waged. The Rev. Martin Luther King, an advocate of nonviolent confrontation against discrimination, had galvanized the movement, and blacks and whites together marched for freedom. King had been involved in the 1955 Montgomery bus boycott after Rosa Parks was arrested for refusing to give up her seat on the bus to a white man. King was often in communication with Kennedy regarding civil rights issues.

The relationship began before Kennedy's presidency when Martin Luther King was arrested for helping students to challenge segregation at a lunch counter in Atlanta. After the arrest, the officials at the jail learned of a bench warrant that had been issued against King; months earlier, King had been charged with driving on an Alabama license although he was living in Georgia. It was during the 1960 campaign, and Kennedy supporters knew that a blatant move of support for King would jeopardize Kennedy's fragile hopes of winning Southern votes. However, his brother-in-law, Sergeant Shriver, gave him Coretta Scott King's telephone number. "I know this must be very hard for you," Kennedy said to Mrs. King, "If there is anything I can do to help, please feel free to call on me."

The gesture, which offended Southern white voters, had a very different effect on black Americans in the South, where the Democratic Party was synonymous with discrimination. When the news leaked out of what Kennedy had done, Kennedy had African-American support. Kennedy had never met Mrs. King, but when asked by a reporter, he said that Mrs. King was a friend.

In June 1963, Alabama's Governor George Wallace, a proponent of segregation now, tomorrow, and forever, personally attempted to prevent students James Hood and Vivian Malone from entering the University of Alabama.

The nation had watched as blacks engaged in nonviolent protests had been greeted with dogs and firehoses. It had learned of blacks being denied the right to vote in elections, of Ku Klux Klan lynch mobs and violent acts of hatred. The nation needed words that would explain the horror of segregation in terms that could inspire hope and change. Kennedy had those words. Explaining his reasons for the legislation he planned to introduce to provide African-Americans with their civil rights, Kennedy, in a televised speech on June 11, 1963, said, "We are confronted primarily with a moral issue. It is as old as the scriptures and is as clear as the American Constitution. . . . One hundred years of delay have passed since President Lincoln freed the slaves, yet their heirs, are not fully free. . . . Now the time has come for this Nation to fulfill its promise."

Kennedy would not live to see the nation fulfill that promise, but the legislation that he sought would become law as the Civil Rights Act of 1964. Lyndon Johnson was committed to the civil rights progress that had begun during JFK's administration, and he had the legislative clout to bring the dream to fruition. What he did not have was the Kennedy mystique, that indescribable ability to captivate the electorate. His own presidency would be shadowed by the violence of the era, the metastasizing spread of the Vietnam War, and the realization that he could not overcome the specter of the martyred president who preceded him.

Chapter Seven

Death in Dallas

"Mr. President, you can't say Dallas doesn't love you!"

—Nellie Connally

By 1963, Kennedy knew that he faced a tough re-election battle and winning Texas was a key factor in his hopes for a second term. Texas Democrats were bickering with one another, but Kennedy knew that he had real enemies in Dallas. One of those foes, Ted Dealey, was the publisher of the *Dallas Morning News*, the newspaper that had published a full-page ad speaking out against JFK's legislative agenda. Kennedy aide Kenny O'Donnell recalled that when Kennedy read the ad, he said to the First Lady, "Oh, you know, we're heading into nut country today. You know, last night would have been a hell of a night to assassinate a President."

The First Lady was not a natural-born campaigner; she was intensely private, preferring to focus on her children and her role as a mother rather than take part in the flesh-pressing aspect of presidential politics. The death of infant Patrick Bouvier Kennedy in August of 1963 had been a devastating blow to Mrs. Kennedy, and recovery had taken its toll on her. She was one of the most admired women in the world, but being the wife of a man who could not be faithful was punishing. However, she decided to join him in Texas and, according to journalist Philip Nobile, the couple had had a reconciliation of sorts by the time they arrived in Dallas. In fact, Nobile reported that author William Manchester, who had interviewed the Kennedy widow extensively while researching his book *The Death of a President,* learned that the First Couple enjoyed a final moment of intimacy during the journey, joining the Mile-High Club aboard Air Force One before the plane landed.

The enthusiastic crowds in Dallas, numbering nearly 200,000 people, saw a radiant First Lady and a smiling President. The Kennedys were traveling in an open convertible with Governor John Connally and his wife, Nellie, who said, "Mr. President, you can't say Dallas doesn't love you," and Kennedy agreed. Those were the last words Kennedy spoke.

The limousine entered Dealey Plaza and continued traveling. When it passed the Texas School Book Depository, shots were fired. Some of the onlookers heard it, but many thought it was backfiring from one of the cars in the procession. Governor Connally would later testify that, as a hunter, he recognized that the noise came from a high-powered rifle. Then bullets struck Connally. Mrs. Conally, hearing the shots, saw President Kennedy's arms move to the front of his face and his throat, and then she heard her husband reacting to being shot. After another shot rang out, Mrs. Connally was hit by the shattered fragments of Kennedy's brain. As the Secret Service agent jumped from the street onto the car, Mrs. Kennedy was climbing onto the back of the car, although she would later not recall doing so.

Mrs. Connally recalled that, during the ride to the hospital, Mrs. Kennedy continued to ask her husband if he could hear her, telling him that she loved him. More than once, she said, "They have killed my husband."

When Kennedy arrived at Parkland Hospital, the staff realized that there was no hope for his survival. Last rites were administered to the deceased President. His body was loaded upon Air Force One for return to Washington D.C. Before the plane left, the oath of office was administered to

Vice President Lyndon B. Johnson; the new First Lady, Lady Bird Johnson, was on one side, the widowed First Lady Jacqueline Kennedy on the other.

For the public, the assassination was numbing, an event that, like the bombing of Pearl Harbor before it and the 9/11 attacks after, branded itself on the nation. People in the streets cried openly as they heard the news; schoolchildren were dismissed from school before the usual time. People feared that the assassination was part of a broader plan to attack the United States. There was fear that the life of the new President was also in danger.

Just over an hour after the assassination, Lee Harvey Oswald was arrested as the murderer of policeman J.D. Tippet. Tippet had recognized Oswald's description from a radio message. When Tippet left his police car, Oswald shot him four times. Oswald tried to slip away unnoticed, but a spectator saw him enter a nearby movie theater. Police arrested him, but Oswald insisted that he had not shot anyone and that the reason he was being arrested was because he had recently been living in the Soviet Union.

Oswald would not live to be tried for the murder. When he was being transferred to the Dallas County Jail two days later, he was shot on live television by nightclub owner Jack Ruby. Oswald, like the president he had killed, was taken to Parkland Hospital, but he could not be saved. Ruby explained that he had killed Oswald to spare Mrs. Kennedy the suffering of having to return to attend the murder trial.

Oswald's death dealt the investigation a crippling blow. Oswald had provided minimal information during the time that he was under interrogation by the Dallas police. Statements that he made, which later were proven to be false, could not be challenged because he was dead. The FBI conducted its own investigation and concluded that the first and third bullets fired hit the President, the second hit the Governor.

On November 29, 1963, President Johnson established the President's Commission on the Assassination of President Kennedy, more familiarly known as the Warren Commission after Chief Justice Earl Warren, who was chairman of the commission. The Commission's 888-page report stated that both Oswald and Ruby had acted alone.

The Commission's report failed to put to rest the conspiracy theories that flourished after Kennedy's assassination. Some believed that the CIA had been behind the killing; others were convinced that Fidel Castro had been involved. Yet another theory held that the Mafia had a hand in the killing. Other commissions conducted investigations but none has been able to solve the lingering mysteries. In 1976, the United States House Select Committee on Assassinations was charged with the investigations of both John F. Kennedy and also Martin Luther King, Jr., who had been assassinated in 1968. The Committee decided that the FBI and CIA had failed to share information with the Warren Commission. The members also stated that the Secret Service had not been sufficiently prepared to provide Kennedy with the level of protection the situation required.

The American public has remained dubious about the official reports, and less than 30% of Americans believe that Oswald acted alone. In 1993, the National Park Service designated the Dealey Plaza site as the Dealey Plaza Historic District, open to the public. The location of Kennedy's limousine at the moment of the shooting is marked with an "X" on the street. More than three hundred thousand visitors visit the Texas School Book Depository, which has a recreation of the area where Oswald set up his post.

The assassination continues to excite interest and inspire controversy. The Kennedy family would remain in the spotlight; Jacqueline Kennedy would marry Greek multimillionaire Aristotle Onassis. Robert Kennedy would also be felled by an assassin's bullet in 1968 when he ran for president. The remaining Kennedy son, Teddy, would mount an unsuccessful presidential campaign in 1980 and then return to the Senate, where he served long enough to create the kind of legislative legacy that his brothers never had the time to fulfill. He was the only one of the four Kennedy sons to die of natural causes.

John Fitzgerald Kennedy, Jr, never had the chance to follow in his father's footsteps, dying in 1999 when the plane he was piloting en route to his cousin's wedding crashed into the Atlantic Ocean. It fell to daughter Caroline to continue the political heritage of her father. In 2013, she was appointed Ambassador to Japan by President Barack Obama.

Other members of the Kennedy clan have followed the family into political office, including the offspring of Robert and Teddy Kennedy. The luster of the Kennedy name may not have the glow that it once had, but it has not faded from public interest.

Jacqueline Kennedy saw her husband's legacy as part of both history and mythology. After his death, she quoted from the lyrics of the musical *Camelot*:

"Don't let it be forgot, that for one brief, shining moment there was Camelot."

Conclusion

She was a woman for whom literature was a lifelong passion, so it was not a surprise for Jacqueline Bouvier Kennedy to view her husband's presidency in metaphorical terms. The glamor and glory of King Arthur's Camelot seemed, to her and to the nation, a fitting symbol for the brief reign of a high-minded president who aspired to do so much, only to be undone by an assassin's bullet. His widow ensured that his funeral would be a fitting farewell to a leader of historical prominence. Despite the weight of her grief and the emotional obligations of a mother to her young children, Mrs. Kennedy built upon the traditional framework of a presidential funeral to customize the ceremony so that it accommodated the historical context of Kennedy's death.

The caisson that carried Kennedy's coffin had also borne the bodies of President Lincoln, himself the victim of an assassin's bullet, and Franklin Roosevelt. Kennedy's three-year-old son saluted the passing of his father's coffin, a moment which touched the hearts of the viewing public. The riderless horse, boots reversed in the stirrups, was in some ways even more memorable a part of the funeral procession than the attendance of the representatives from the eighty-two nations who came.

Perhaps the most significant feature of the funeral was the eternal flame which was placed at the president's grave at Arlington Cemetery. That symbol of eternal light would illuminate the legacy of a man who is ranked high, decades after his death, by Americans but not so by historians.

How would Kennedy have handled the fissures in American society which seemed to indicate that the country was undergoing a second Civil War? Violence, protests against the Vietnam War; drugs, civil rights, changing roles for women, the peace movement, and a sense that there was an inherent schism dividing Americans dominated the headlines.

The decade came to a close with a reminder of Kennedy's legacy. In May 1961, Kennedy spoke before a joint session of Congress that an American would set foot on the moon and be returned safely to Earth before the 1960s ended. It was a bold proclamation, one uttered as part of the subtext of competition between the United States and the Soviet Union. It did not seem likely that such an enormous project could possibly be completed in so short a time, but on July 20, 1969, Apollo 11 astronaut Neil Armstrong made Kennedy's prediction come true when he landed on the surface of the moon.

Perhaps that, more than any of the other events of Kennedy's time in office, most fittingly describes his legacy. He was a president who encouraged Americans to ask what they could do for their country. He inspired Americans, and many citizens of other countries as well, to reach for the moon.